GREAT
MONUMENTS
OF INDIA

Publisher : **MELROY DICKSON**
Photographer : **RUPINDER KHULLAR**
Text : **REETA KHULLAR**
Designer : **YOGESH GAJWANI**

Published by India Book Distributors
(Bombay) Ltd.,
1007/1008 Arcadia, 195 Nariman Point,
Bombay 400 021
Tel. : 22 46 46/22 46 91/287 25 28/
287 25 32.
Telex : 011-86085 IBD IN
Fax : 022-287 25 31

ISBN 81-7310-025-X

Printed at Thomson Press (India) Ltd.

GREAT
MONUMENTS
OF INDIA
·

RUPINDER KHULLAR
REETA KHULLAR

The cultural heritage of India's five thousand-year-old civilisation is manifest in the monuments scattered across the length and breadth of the country. These forts, palaces, *stupas*, temples, mosques and towers show that India's architectural tradition has always been a living form of expression. The sculptural and decorative details provide ·vital information and insights into the social, political, religious and artistic history of the country.

The earliest existing evidence of building activity can be traced back to Mohenjodaro and the Harappan cities of the Indus river valley in 2500 B.C. Here archaeological excavations have unearthed meticulously planned towns with well laid out streets and a proper drainage system, making them the earliest urban cities in history.

We have very little information regarding the centuries that followed. The next great period of building and sculptural activity occurred during the time of the Mauryan dynasty. Buddhism gained momentum and flourished under the Mauryas in the third century B.C. and commemorative monuments in stone began to be constructed for the first time. They could be categorised into three basic forms, the *stupa*, the *chaitya* and the *vihara*. The *stupa*, originally a hemispherical funerary mound, is one of the earliest religious architectural forms in India. The Sanchi stupa built by Mauryan Emperor

Ashoka is a beautiful example of this form. The *chaityas* were congregational halls sometimes carved out of living rock as at Karla, and the *viharas* were monasteries and centres of Buddhist learning. The rock cut technique and the use of stone pillars and beams may still be seen at the rock cut caves at Karla, Bhaja, Ajanta and Ellora in the western state of Maharashtra. The twenty-nine caves at Ajanta dating from the second century B.C. to the tenth century B.C. possess an unparalleled treasure of painting, sculpture and architecture. A study of the Ajanta caves reveals the entire evolution of Buddhist architecture.

The next great period of building activity took place during the reign of the great Gupta emperors in the third, fourth and fifth centuries A.D. There was a resurgence of Hindu thought during this period resulting in the development of a style of temple architecture which has become the most characteristic form of India's sacred architecture. The Hindu temple was conceived as an abode of the Gods and the early temple was a single square sanctum with the main image installed in it.

With the fall of the Gupta empire, several small kingdoms came into existence. Over the centuries this lead to the evolution of a more elaborate regional architectural style. The Chalukya kings who ruled over a large portion of south India, built a series of cave temples based on *chaitya* and *vihara* forms in Aihole and Badami from the sixth century onwards. The temple spire or the *shikara* became an important feature of the Hindu temple. In north and central India, the *shikara* was shaped like an upturned cone while in the south Indian temples the *shikara* was more like a stepped pyramid. In the eighth century A.D., the Pallavas added yet another dimension to rock cut architecture with temples made out of granite such as the Mahabalipuram shore temple, which, in turn, served as a model for the Virupaksha temple in Pattadakal and the Kailashnath temple at Ellora.

In north and central India, temple architecture reached its zenith in the centuries that followed. The Orissa temples, built in the unique *Nagara* style, had a tall primary structure with a soaring convex spire and a cubical inner sanctum.

The stylistic development of the Orissa temples, beginning with the seventh century Parasurameswara temple at Bhubaneswar, had many significant creations such as the Lingaraja temple, also at Bhubaneswar and the Jagannath temple at Puri, till it reached a climax in the chariot-shaped Sun temple at Konarak built in the thirteenth century.

The finest examples of the Khajuraho style of temples, built by the Chandellas in the eleventh and twelfth centuries, are the Kandariya Mahadev and the Parsvanatha temples. Unlike the multi-unit temples of Orissa, these consist of one compact unified unit standing on a lofty platform.

Around this time, the Hoysala rulers in the south were building profusely carved star-shaped shrines in Belur, Halebid and Somnathpur in the modern—day state of Karnataka. Further south, in what is now Tamil Nadu, the temple became the nucleus of the entire city as in Madurai, Srirangam and Rameswaram. The main features of these monumental structures were their awe inspiring *gopurams* and long corridors lined with intricately carved pillars.

The last great example of the Hindu temple can be seen in the medieval ruins at Hampi. The famous Virupaksha temple and the Vithala temple (with its musical pillars and monolithic chariot) were built by the Vijayanagar kings who ruled over a magnificent empire in the fifteenth and sixteenth centuries A.D.

The temples built by the followers of the Jain faith followed the concept of the Hindu temples. The main deity was enshrined in the inner sanctum, which was surmounted by a spire. The earliest Jain temples were cave shrines found in places where Jainism first took root such as Bihar, Orissa and south India. Some outstanding creations of Jain architecture may be seen at the Ellora complex. The colossal 17−metre high statue of Jain saint Lord Gomateshwara in Sravanabelagola is considered one of the tallest monolithic statues in the world. It is, however, the Jain temples at Mt. Abu and Ranakpur in Rajasthan, dedicated to Jain Tirthankaras that remain unrivalled in their superb architecture and profusion of sculptural ornamentation.

Following the Muslim invasions into India towards the end of the twelfth century A.D., Qutubuddin Aibak became the first of the Sultans who ruled from what is now Delhi. The new dynasty brought to India elements of the architecture of their homeland. Features like arches, domes, minarets and kiosks were part of the new architectural style which found expression in monumental mosques, minars, tombs and fortified palaces.

The Qutub Minar, built by Qutubuddin Aibak was the first Indo-Islamic monument built according to a formal plan. It remains unsurpassed even today.

Building activity under subsequent dynasties such as the Khaljis, the Tughlaqs and the Lodhis was impressive and it was during this period that the hemispherical dome evolved. This characteristic form was used in mosques, tombs and palaces. The Mughals came to power in the sixteenth century and they took Islamic architecture in India to sublime heights. Humayun's Tomb, with its bulbous marble dome and well laid out gardens is considered an important landmark in Mughal architecture. Emperor Akbar's building style was unique and all embracing like his personality. He favoured a beautiful blend of indigenous Hindu and Persian ideas and this is evident in Fatehpur Sikri, the city he built outside Agra, and in his tomb at Sikandra.

While Jahangir, Akbar's son, made painting an integral part of Mughal ornamentation as is amply evident at Itmad-ud-Daulah's Tomb in Agra, it was Shah Jahan whose contribution to architecture is remembered most vividly. He used white marble instead of red sandstone and was successful in introducing new features such as engraved arches, double domes and curved cornices in the monuments he built at the Agra fort, the Red Fort and the Jama Masjid in Delhi. However, it was his creation of the Taj Mahal that took Mughal architecture to its pinnacle, a befitting example of a glorious era in Indian architecture spanning almost five hundred years.

Early British influence on Indian architecture followed the inroads of the London East India Company into India. Initially, they set up trade centres or factories which had an entirely simple and utilitarian style. While the British in the beginning concentrated on places like Calcutta, Bombay and Madras, the Portuguese established their base in Goa and the French in Pondicherry.

All this changed when the British consolidated their power over a large part of India, and Queen Victoria was proclaimed the Empress of India in 1876. The British began to build impressive government buildings, courts and forts in the imperial style. They created a curious synthesis of architectural designs from Rome, Greece and Europe with Indian embellishments.

New Delhi, the capital, designed by the British and the other big cities like Bombay, Calcutta and Madras are examples of British colonial architecture in India.

The city of Chandigarh designed by French architect Corbusier sowed the seeds of modern Indian architecture in the post Independence era.

As things stand today, Indian architects are striving for a contemporary style that is functional, modern and yet rooted in the traditions of the past.

THIKSE MONASTERY, LADAKH. The Thikse Monastery in Ladakh is known for its splendid architecture. It houses a beautiful image of the Buddha. Left: LAMAYURU MONASTERY, Ladakh. The Lamayuru Buddhist monastery is venerated as the oldest religious centre in Ladakh. Situated at a height of 4,000 metres, the monastery overlooks the Indus river.

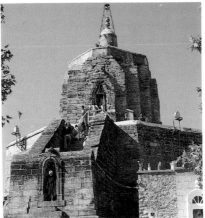

Left : VAISHNODEVI, JAMMU. The cave shrine at Vaishnodevi in the Trikuta mountains is one of the most important pilgrimage centres for Hindus. Devotees trek fourteen kilometres up the mountain to worship at natural rock formations that represent the divine aspects of the goddesses Kali, Lakshmi and Saraswati. Left below: SHANKARACHARYA TEMPLE, KASHMIR. The Shankaracharya Temple, built around 200 BC, is dedicated to Lord Shiva. Situated on top of the Takht-i-Sulaiman hill, it commands a spectacular view of Srinagar and its surroundings. Opposite Page: AMAR MAHAL, JAMMU, The Amar Mahal is situated in the heart of Jammu, a city in the foothills of the Himalayas. Built by Raja Amar Singh, this elegantly designed palace is in the French style.

Right : BADRINATH, UTTAR PRADESH. The Badrinath shrine dedicated to Lord Vishnu, is one of the four dhams or sacred places of pilgrimage for Hindus. Right below : LAXMI NARAYAN TEMPLES, CHAMBA, HIMACHAL PRADESH. The Laxmi Narayan complex at Chamba in the Himalayas, is built on a high terrace above the confluence of two rivers. These single storeyed stone temples have carved decorative motifs on their outer walls while the interiors have brass sculptures inlaid with silver and copper. Opposite Page: GOLDEN TEMPLE, AMRITSAR, PUNJAB. The Golden temple in Amritsar is the most hallowed of Sikh shrines. The sixteenth century temple stands in the middle of the Amrita Sarovar (or pool of nectar). The holy book of the Sikhs, the Guru Granth Sahib occupies a place of honour on a bejewelled throne on the ground floor.

Above : The IRON PILLAR, QUTUB COMPLEX, NEW DELHI.
The fourth century iron pillar in the Qutub complex
is believed to have been placed here by the Sultan of
Delhi because of its superb craftsmanship. The very
fact that it has remained rust free for more than
sixteen hundred years speaks volumes for the skill of
Indian metallurgists of ancient times. Right :   A
beautiful example of Islamic calligraphy in the
Qutub complex. Opposite page QUTUB MINAR, NEW
DELHI. Built of red sandstone in the Islamic style, the
Qutub Minar is a landmark in the capital of the
country.

Above : RASHTRAPATI BHAVAN, NEW DELHI. Rashtrapati Bhavan is the official residence of the President of India. Earlier known as the Viceregal lodge, this important twentieth century building was designed by Sir Lutyens in the 1920's. Top: The BAHAI TEMPLE, NEW DELHI. The Bahai faith, the world's youngest religion, is represented in India by the magnificent Bahai temple built in 1986 in the shape of a blossoming lotus. Opposite page : INDIA GATE, NEW DELHI. The All India War Memorial, generally called India Gate is an arch commemorating nearly 70,000 soldiers who died in World War I. It was designed by Sir Lutyens in 1931. An eternal flame called the Amar Jawan Jyoti dedicated to the unknown soldier was placed under the arch after the Indo–Pakistan War of 1971.

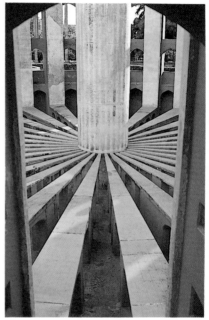

Above : JANTAR MANTAR, NEW DELHI. This observatory was built by Maharaja Sawai Jai Singh II of Jaipur in 1724. A keen astronomer, the Maharaja built five such observatories at different locations to help him to formulate astronomical studies. Left: HUMAYUN'S TOMB, NEW DELHI. The mausoleum of the second Mughal emperor, Humayun was built in 1564 by his widow Haji Begum during her son Akbar's reign. It is considered a forerunner to the perfect proportions of the celebrated Taj Mahal.

21

JAMA MASJID, DELHI. The Jama Masjid is one of the largest and most beautiful mosques in India. It was built in 1650–56 by Mughal Emperor Shah Jahan on a small hillock opposite the Red Fort.

Above : DIWAN–E–AM, RED FORT, DELHI. The Diwan–e–Am or the hall of public audience is a flat roofed hall with rows of beautiful cusped arches. The emperor's throne was placed in an alcove in the back walls of the hall. Top : RED FORT, DELHI. The Fifth Mughal Emperor Shah Jahan built the Red Fort on the banks of river Yamuna when he shifted his capital from Agra to Shahjahanabad in 1638. The massive fort, made in red sandstone, is an irregular octagon in shape, with high battlemented walls.

The TAJ MAHAL, AGRA. The Taj Mahal was built by Mughal Emperor Shah Jahan on the banks of river Yamuna in the seventeenth century in memory of his wife Mumtaz. This monument of love was made possible by the superb craftsmanship of twenty thousand workers who worked day and night for seventeen years. Inset: The Taj is decorated with intricate marble inlay work, like this panel. Following page: The FORT, AGRA, This imposing citadel built of red sandstone and marble spans the history of three emperors. It was originally planned as a fortified military structure by Akbar but by the time it was completed in Shah Jahan's reign, it had acquired all the trimmings of an imperial palace.

Above : ITMAD-UD DAULLAH'S TOMB, AGRA. This serene marble mausoleum was built by Jehangir's wife Nur Jahan in 1626 in memory of her father. This tomb marks the beginning of the use of white marble in place of red sandstone. The profuse ornamentation with mosaic and pietra-dura inlay work adds a touch of delicacy to the splendid monument.
Top : SIKANDRA, AGRA. The elegant tomb of Emperor Akbar situated eight kilometres from Agra, is a harmonious combination of Hindu and Muslim architectural styles. It is a five storeyed building with the real tomb in the basement below and a decorated tombstone built exactly over it on the top floor.

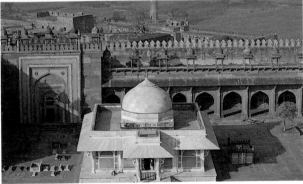

Above : SALIM CHISTI'S TOMB, FATEHPUR SIKRI. The tomb of Sheikh Salim Chisti, a sufi saint, is the heart of Fatehpur Sikri. Emperor Akbar chose this spot to build his new city because Salim Chisti had his hermitage here. He had the tomb built after the saint's death in 1572. It is now a place of pilgrimage venerated by both Hindus and Muslims. Top : The PANCH MAHAL, FATEHPUR SIKRI. This is a five storeyed pavilion with successive floors of diminishing size with an open pavillion at the top which provides a magnificent view of the imperial capital city built by Emperor Akbar. It is situated forty kilometres from Agra.

VISHWANATH TEMPLE, VARANASI, UTTAR PRADESH.
The Vishwanath golden temple is the nucleus
around which life in Varanasi revolves. The
present temple was rebuilt on the original site by
Maratha Queen Ahilya Bai in 1776. Lord Shiva,
the chief deity of the shrine is symbolically
represented here by a black stone lingam.
Below : SARNATH, UTTAR PRADESH. A
contemporary wall painting depicting the
miracle of the thousand Buddhas at Sarnath.

Left : SARNATH, UTTAR PRADESH. An image of Buddha (4th–5thC) preaching his first sermon at the Deer Park at Sarnath. A symbol of the Buddhist wheel of law, believed to have been set in motion by him is visible on the lower part of the image. Below : DHAMEKH STUPA, SARNATH UTTAR PRADESH. Sarnath, situated eight kilometres from Varanasi, is an important Buddhist place of pilgrimage because Lord Buddha preached his first sermon here. The famous Dhamekh Stupa constructed by the great Maurya King Ashoka in the third century BC is considered the most important structure at Sarnath.

JAISALMER FORT, RAJASTHAN. The fort at Jaisalmer rises like a golden mirage from the desert sands. The seventy six metre high fort was constructed by a Rajput Chief Jaisal in 1156. It is built of yellow sandstone which takes on a golden hue at sunrise.

MEHERANGARH FORT, JODHPUR, RAJASTHAN. The impregnable Meherangarh Fort was built in 1459 by Rao Jodha. The magnificent palaces within the fort are protected by seven massive gates. Top : MEHERANGARH FORT, JODHPUR, RAJASTHAN. The Phool Mahal or the Flower Palace, built by Maharaja Abhai Singh in the eighteenth century is famous for its gold work and intricately painted patterns.

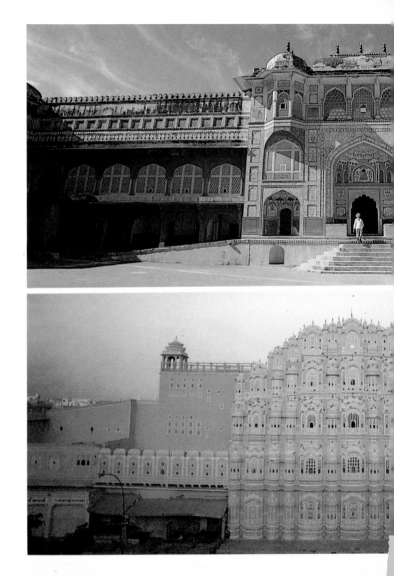

Left below : HAWA MAHAL, JAIPUR, RAJASTHAN:
The Hawa Mahal or the Palace of Winds is
actually just an extraordinary facade in pink
sandstone. This five storey structure with 953
secluded niches decorated with pierced
stone screens and carved balconies was used
by the royal women to watch the outside
world from the seclusion of 'Purdah'. Left
above : AMBER FORT, JAIPUR, RAJASTHAN.
It was constructed by Raja Man Singh I in 1592
and was the state capital for six centuries, before
the city of Jaipur was built. The impressive
Ganesh Pol with colourful images is the
ceremonial gateway leading to the royal
apartments. Amber just eleven kilometres from
Jaipur is famous for its picturesque setting.

35

Above left: RANAKPUR TEMPLES, RAJASTHAN. Nearly one hundred and sixty kilometres north-west from Udaipur lie another group of magnificent Jain temples at Ranakpur. Built by a wealthy Jain merchant in the fifteenth century, the main Chaumukha temple is dedicated to Jain Tirthankara Adinath. The temple built on a high plinth has more than a thousand elaborately carved pillars. The temple has five shrines covered by spires and cupolas and the central shrine has a white marble image of Chaumukha, the chief deity. Above right: DILWARA TEMPLES, MOUNT ABU, RAJASTHAN. The famous Dilwara temples in Mount Abu are an important centre of pilgrimage for followers of the Jain faith. The temples built of pure white marble, are carved with so much intricate detail that the effect is of light and airy delicacy. The two main shrines are the Adinath temple built in 1031 and dedicated to the first Jain Tirthankara or teacher and Neminath constructed in 1230 dedicated to the twenty second Tirthankara. Opposite page: SUN TEMPLE, MODHERA, GUJARAT. The Sun temple at Modhera, situated a hundred and four kilometres from Ahmedabad was built in AD 1026 by King Bhimdev I of the Solanki dynasty. The temple dedicated to the Sun God Surya, was partly destroyed by invaders but its architectural grandeur is still evident.

PARSVANATH TEMPLE,
KHAJURAHO, MADHYA PRADESH. This panel
of sculpture depicts a woman decorating
her feet with a red dye called 'alta', a
tradition still followed by women in
some parts of the country.

Above : PARSVANATH TEMPLE, KHAJURAHO, MADHYA PRADESH. An elegant sculpture of Laxmi Narayan (Lord Vishnu with his consort Lakshmi) from the Parsvanath temple. Left : VISHVANATH TEMPLE, KHAJURAHO, MADHYA PRADESH. The Vishvanath temple built in AD 1002 is one of the finest temples of Khajuraho. It is built on a platform which it shares with a shrine dedicated to Shiva's mount, the bull Nandi. The temple shows a marked maturity in terms of plan and design in Khajuraho temple architecture.

Above : STUPA, SANCHI, MADHYA PRADESH. The great stupa at Sanchi, built by Emperor Ashoka, remains the best preserved stupa in India. It is a hemispherical dome 36.5 metres in diameter and is surrounded by a stone railing interspersed with gateways. Top: NALANDA, Bihar. About eighty kilometres from Patna lie the ruins of Nalanda, a celebrated seat of learning during the Gupta period in the seventh century. Among the thousands who received education on the Mahayana doctrine of Buddhism here, was the famous Chinese traveller Hieun Tsang.

Opposite page: MAHABODHI TEMPLE, BODHGAYA, BIHAR. Bodhgaya is revered by Buddhist pilgrims from all over the world, because this is where the Buddha is believed to have attained enlightenment. The famous Mahabodhi temple facing the site was built in the 2nd century. (Inset). The 'diamond throne' created by the gods, upon which Sakyamuni, the Buddha-to-be, is said to have spread his seat of grass and meditated until he finally attained enlightenment.

Above : DAKSHINESHWAR TEMPLE, CALCUTTA, WEST
BENGAL. The Dakshineshwar temple complex six
kilometers from Calcutta was built in 1855 by a
wealthy and devout widow named Rani Rashmoni. The
most famous shrine here is the Kali temple.
Opposite page: VICTORIA MEMORIAL CALCUTTA, WEST
BENGAL. The Victoria Memorial, built of white marble
was an important symbol of British power in
India. It was inaugurated by the Prince of Wales in
1921 and houses paintings, a collection of Victorian
memorabilia and objects and documents concerning
the history of Bengal.

Above and Right: LINGARAJA TEMPLE, BHUBANESHWAR, ORISSA. The Lingaraja temple towers high over the city. Built in AD 1114, it is an impressive example of Orissa temple architecture. The main deity is Tribhuvaneswar, Lord of the three worlds and He is portrayed as being both Lord Shiva and Lord Vishnu.

Above and Left: JAGANNATH TEMPLE, PURI, ORISSA. This twelfth century temple, built by king Choda Gangadeva is dedicated to Lord Jagannath or Lord of the Universe represented in a Trinity with his brother Balbhadra and his sister Subhadra. It is one of Hinduism's holiest shrines. The Jagannath cult permeates almost every aspect of life in Puri and the climax is reached in the Rath Yatra festival when the deities are taken out in huge wooden chariots in July every year.

45

SUN TEMPLE KONARK, ORISSA. The magnificent Sun temple at Konark was built by King Narasimhadeva in the thirteenth century. Shaped like a colossal stone chariot, carrying the sun god Surya across the sky, the temple marks the culmination of Orissa temple architecture. The twelve wheels of the chariot symbolise the twelve months of the year, while the seven horses pulling the chariot signify the number of days in a week.

AJANTA CAVES, MAHARASHTRA. These rock-cut caves set deep in the Sahyadri hills near Aurangabad offer an unmatched visual treat of painting, sculpture and architectural design. Images of royal life and,the lives of humble people, depiction of the Buddhist Jataka tales embody the inspiration and devotion of the Buddhist Monks who created these extraordinary works of art in ancient times.

Above : AJANTA CAVES, MAHARASHTRA. This large relief shows the
death of the Buddha. He lies on a bed placed between two sala
trees with his head facing the north. The scriptures say that he
lay on his right side and addressed his followers for the last
time. Top: AJANTA CAVES, MAHARASHTRA. A mural depicting
courtly life.

Above : ELEPHANTA, MAHARASHTRA. The Elephanta Caves are situated on an island some nine kilometres from Bombay. These seventh century rock cut cave temples are renowned for their exquisite carvings depicting the Shiva myths. Pulakesin II of the Chalukya kingdom is said to have constructed this shrine in AD 634. Left: ELLORA, MAHARASHTRA. The thirty four cave temples at Ellora have intricate interiors and ornamental facades. Carved during the fifth and eighth century AD, the rock temples and monasteries here represent the three faiths of Hinduism, Buddhism and Jainism. These caves are situated thirty kilometres from Aurangabad.

51

THE BASILICA OF BOM JESUS

VELHA, GOA. The church of Bom Jesus in Velha, Goa originally built in 1560 is a mixture of Portuguese and Gothic architecture. The church is famous because it enshrines the miraculously incorruptible body of St. Francis Xavier in a beautiful marble and silver casket.

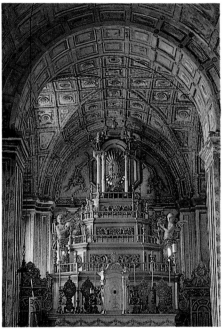

THE SE CATHEDRAL, VELHA GOA.
The Se'Cathedral dedicated to St. Catherine of
Alexandria was built in 1562. The interior of the
cathedral is adorned with gold stucco reliefs and
paintings representing Indo – Portuguese art.

VITHALA TEMPLE, HAMPI, KARNATAKA: An extraordinary example of sculptural skill, this temple is a stone replica of a temple chariot, with wheels that actually rotate. The exterior is intricately carved and decorated. The temple is dedicated to Lord Vishnu. Opposite page: HAMPI, KARNATAKA: The ruined capital of the great sixteenth century Vijaynagar kingdom may be seen at Hampi in Karnataka. Palaces, temples, baths, stables and other structures are scattered across a dramatic landscape beside the Tungabhadra river. The sacred Virupaksha temple, built in medieval Deccan style and dedicated to Lord Shiva and his consort is still used as a place of worship.

Above : CHENNA KESAVA VISHNU TEMPLE, BELUR, KARNATAKA. The Chenna Kesava Vishnu temple in Belur is an exquisite example of Hoysala architecture. It was built in commemoration of Hoysala king Vishnuvardhana's victory over the Cholas in AD 1117. The temple reveals itself like a series of stories in stone with intricately carved interior and exterior. Top: KESAVA TEMPLE, SOMNATHPUR, KARNATAKA. This star shaped temple, dedicated to Lord Vishnu was built by Somnath, a Hoysala minister in the thirteenth century. A fine example of Hoysala architecture, the temple is profusely decorated with panels of intricate sculptures.

Above : HOYSALESVARA TEMPLE, HALEBID, KARNATAKA. The famous twelfth century Hoysalesvara temple in Halebid is one hundred and eighty kilometres from Bangalore. This temple marks the pinnacle of Hoysala artistic creation. Top: SRAVANABELAGOLA, KARNATAKA. Sravanabelagola, one hundred and seventy kilometres from Bangalore is famous for its colossal monolithic statue of Lord Gomateshwara built in AD 980. It is a place of pilgrimage to followers of the Jain faith. The Mahamastabhisheka ceremony held every twelve years, draws thousands of devotees from every part of the country.

Above : DURBAR HALL, MAHARAJA'S PALACE, MYSORE. The Durbar Hall, where the Maharaja received visitors is profusely and extravagantly decorated. Top: AMBA VILAS, MAHARAJA'S PALACE, MYSORE. This sumptuously decorated hall characterises the opulence of the Palace. Opposite page: THE MAHARAJA'S PALACE, MYSORE, KARNATAKA. The Palace, built in the late nineteenth century by the Wadeyars is a superb example of the Indo-Saracenic school of architecture. The exterior has cupolas, minarets, domes and balconies embellished with detailed carvings. It is still the residence of the erstwhile royal family.

Below : GOLCONDA FORT, ANDHRA PRADESH. The formidable Golconda fort, situated eleven kilometres from Hyderabad is located at a height of almost 120 metres. The fort and the monuments in and around it still stand testimony to the aura of power and grandeur that surrounded the Qutb Shahi monarchs of the sixteenth century. Left: TIRUPATI, ANDHRA PRADESH. The Tirupati shrine situated on the crest of one of seven hills is dedicated to Lord Vishnu or Venkateswara. All the activities of the town centre around this 2000-year-old temple. Tirupati is believed to be the richest and busiest shrine in the world. Opposite page: CHARMINAR, HYDERABAD, ANDHRA PRADESH. The magnificent Charminar built in 1591 is the most important landmark in the city of Hyderabad.

61

MAHABALIPURAM, TAMIL NADU: A masterpiece of Indian art can be seen at Mahabalipuram in the form of the world's largest bas–relief. On a huge outcrop of fissured rock, artists sculpted a beautiful composition of human and celestial beings and animals depicting 'ARJUNA'S PENANCE' or THE DESCENT OF THE GANGA' Opposite page: SHORE TEMPLE, MAHABALIPURAM, TAMIL NADU. The shore temple in Mahabalipuram was built by Pallava King Nandi Varman II in the eighth century and represents the final phase of Pallava art. Besides its ornamentation, exquisite sculpture and perfect proportions, the temple is unique because it includes shrines dedicated to both Lord Shiva and Lord Vishnu.

GOL GUMBAZ, BIJAPUR, KARNATAKA. The Gol Gumbaz in Bijapur is famous for its enormous dome which measures 2.8 metres in diameter and is second only to St. Peter's in Rome in size. The mausoleum of Mohammed Adil Shah built in 1659 during his own lifetime represents the architectural austerity of the Adil Shahi style. Opposite page, above: BADAMI, KARNATAKA. The Vishnu cave is a fine example of sixth century Chalukyan architecture. The interior has a four armed figure of Lord Vishnu seated on the serpent Ananth Naga. Below: PATTADAKAL, KARNATAKA. The temple city of Pattadakal thirty kilometres from Badami was the last capital of the Chalukya rulers. The cluster of beautiful temples belonging to the seventh and eighth century are constructed in a mixture of north Indian and south Indian styles and depict the progression in style and structure from the Badami temples.

VADAKKUNATHAN TEMPLE, TRICHUR, KERALA. The main deity of the shrine is Lord Shiva. The temple exterior built of wood with low tiled roofs is simple and typical of Kerala architecture. The temple is famous for its spectacular Pooram festival held in April/May every year.
Right: RAMESWARAM TEMPLE, TAMIL NADU. The Rameswaram temple situated on an island in the Gulf of Mannar is one of the holiest places of pilgrimage for Hindus. The temple, which was completed in 350 years, is associated with Lord Ram. The temple is famed for its kilometre -long pillared corridor which surrounds the main quadrangle.

SRIRANGAPATNAM, KARNATAKA . Sixteen kilometres from Mysore is the erstwhile capital city of the great Tipu Sultan and the scene of many heroic battles. He was buried in 1799 beside the tombs of his family members in the Gumbaz. It is an impressive structure with a beautiful dome and four minarets, reminiscent of the Taj Mahal.

SRIRANGAM, TIRUCHIRAPALLI, TAMIL NADU. The Srirangam temple is located on an island formed by the Kaveri and Kollidam rivers. It is the largest of the Dravidian temples and was built during the 16 century AD by the Nayakas. It is dedicated to Lord Vishnu who is depicted in a reclining posture on his five hooded serpent Adisesha. The main feature of the temple is the Hall of a Thousand Pillars, some of which are exquisitely carved.

Opposite page: BRIHADEESWARAR TEMPLE, THANJAVUR, TAMIL NADU. The Brihadeeswarar temple, dedicated to Lord Shiva was built by Raja Raja Chola in the eleventh century. It is undoubtedly the most magnificent creation of Chola art because of its perfect symmetry. The awe - inspiring 66 metre temple tower built of granite is considered an architectural marvel.

VIVEKANANDA ROCK MEMORIAL, KANYAKUMARI. The memorial dedicated to Swami
Vivekananda is built on a rock 1200 metres from the shore at the southern tip of the Indian
Peninsula. The Arabian Sea, the Bay of Bengal and the Indian Ocean meet here. Swami
Vivekananda meditated here on this rocky outcrop in 1892 before he travelled to the west
with his philosophy of Vedanta. A shrine dedicated to the virgin goddess Kanya Kumari is
also located here and is a place of pilgrimage for devout Hindus. Preceding page:
MEENAKSHI TEMPLE, MADURAI, TAMIL NADU. Almost all activities in the temple city of Madurai
are oriented towards the colossal Meenakshi temple built in sixteenth century by Pandyan
rulers. The temple is renowned for its gopurams and for its lotus tank beside the temples.
The Ayirakkar Mandapam with its thousand pillared hall is one of the complex's most
distinguished features. The temple is dedicated to Lord Shiva's consort the goddess
Meenakshi.